FALCON WATCH

by Jesse Beecher

Scott Foresman

Editorial Offices: Glenview, Illinois • New York, New York
Sales Offices: Reading, Massachusetts • Duluth, Georgia
Glenview, Illinois • Carrollton, Texas • Menlo Park, California

A bird circles above me. It dives toward the cliff. Then it disappears into a crack in the rock. Another bird shoots out. Then it flies away. I can't see the bird in the cliff. But I know that it must be sitting on eggs.

Each spring, falcons scratch a nest in a cave on this cliff. The female lays two to five eggs in it.

The parent birds sit on the eggs to keep them warm. It takes five weeks for most varieties to hatch. While one bird sits, the other hunts.

When a falcon hunts, it dives through the air as fast as 150 miles an hour. It strikes a smaller bird on the back. Then it brings the bird back to the nest. Sometimes, it eats the kill itself.

Falcons don't always nest on cliffs. They also nest on buildings in cities.

Suppose you are a falcon. You fly to a big city. You look at the tall buildings. You think, "What high cliffs. I'm fond of cliffs. Why don't I live here?"

That's what some falcons do. There are many different varieties of falcons in big cities across the country.

I started watching falcons when I was twelve. My librarian told me that the Audubon Society needed people to help study falcons. She told me that she was fond of falcons too! So I called Mr. Martin at the Audubon Society. He said there were falcons at Square Ledge. This cliff is near my home in the White Mountains of New Hampshire.

Mr. Martin told me how to watch the birds through a spotting scope. He said my bird watching would help us find out if the falcons had chicks. That year I promised to hike three miles to the cliff every week. There I would watch the birds.

The first time, I hiked through three feet of snow. I had to use snowshoes. One week in April, I saw moose and bear tracks. When the snow melted, the place was buzzing with many varieties of mosquitoes!

Sometimes, I hiked with my friends. Other times my parents went with me.

Each time I reached the cliff, I set up the scope. I listened. I watched. I wrote notes.

Often the falcons were out of sight. They were hunting or sitting on the eggs. I spent most of my time waiting.

Finally, in May, I knew the eggs had hatched. I could tell because the parents were so busy. They brought food to the nest to feed their young.

I still didn't know how many chicks there were. I couldn't see into the nest. It was too high.

When I went back, I watched two climbers reach Square Ledge. They were going to check on the chicks.

I held my breath. "How many chicks will there be?"

Through the scope, I saw the climbers lift one egg.

"Oh no," I said. "That one didn't hatch."

But then they found two white, screeching chicks.

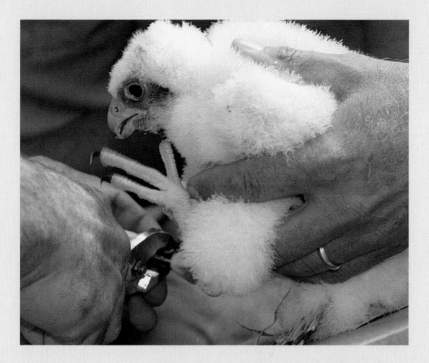

The climbers put a small band around each chick's leg. The leg bands help watchers identify these birds.

They took pictures of the nest. They collected feathers. And they took parts of prey the falcons had eaten. They sent the unhatched egg to a lab. There, scientists would try to figure out why it didn't hatch.

In the 1960s, there were no falcons nesting east of the Mississippi River. This was because of DDT. DDT was sprayed to kill insects. DDT made the eggshells of birds break easily. In 1972, DDT was banned in the United States. But falcons were still in danger. That is why I helped study them.

My work that spring was done. Before I left, I took one last look at Square Ledge. I caught a glimpse of a falcon high in the air. I smiled as I thought how fond I am of these birds. There were two new falcons in the world!

"Goodbye. I'll see you again next year."